AVENUE OF VANISHING

AVENUE OF

VANISHING

WILLIAM OLSEN

TriQuarterly Books
Northwestern University Press
Evanston, Illinois

TriQuarterly Books
Northwestern University Press
www.nupress.northwestern.edu

Printed in the United States of America

10 9 8 7 6 5 4 3 2 1

ISBN-13: 978-0-8101-5181-9 (cloth)
ISBN-10: 0-8101-5181-2 (cloth)
ISBN-13: 978-0-8101-5182-6 (paper)
ISBN-10: 0-8101-5182-0 (paper)

Library of Congress Cataloging-in-Publication Data

Olsen, William, 1954–
    Avenue of vanishing / William Olsen.
      p. cm.
    Includes bibliographical references.
    ISBN-13: 978-0-8101-5181-9 (cloth : alk. paper)
    ISBN-13: 978-0-8101-5182-6 (pbk. : alk. paper)
    I. Title.
    PS3565.L822A95 2007
    811.54—dc22
                                        2006102079

♾ The paper used in this publication meets the
minimum requirements of the American National Standard
for Information Sciences—Permanence of Paper for
Printed Library Materials, ANSI Z39.48-1984.

Contents

Acknowledgments

Grateful acknowledgments to the editors of the following journals, where some of these poems appeared, sometimes in different versions:

Alaska Quarterly: "Pretty Soon They'll Hear the Suitcase of My Heart," as "Birth Day Blues"

American Literary Review: " 'Tis of Thee"

Georgia Review: "By a Railroad Crossing"

Gettysburg Review: "Ease," "The Managerial Sublime," "The World Below"

Gulf Coast: "Sotto Voce," as "Silence Has No Vocabulary to Speak Of"

Indiana Review: "Gegenschein: 1959"

Lit Rag: "False Rue"

The Literary Review: "Creation Assumes the Form of Washed-Up Kelp"

Paris Review: section 2 of "Commotions," as "Out of Love"

Parthenon West: "The Book of Love," "Phone Book," "Universe of Fear"

Ploughshares: "Infinity"

Poetry: "A Fallen Bat"

Poetry Miscellany: "Blood"

Saranac Review: "All Moon"

Shade: "Avenue of Vanishing," as "Success"

Shenandoah: "Frost's Last Lecture: A Tape: His Audience"

Southern Review: sections 1 and 3 of "Commotions," as "Cornish Crows" and "Penwith Crows"

TriQuarterly: "A Few of the Many Numbered Birds of the State of Oaxaca,"
  "All-American," "Neither Paradise nor Below, nor Up nor Down,"
  "Rag for the Prayer-Rag Tree," as "Rag for the Cornish Prayer Rag Tree,"
  "Study of the Resurrection"

Western Humanities Review: section 3 of "Commotions," as "Nova Scotia Snapshot
  Lying on the Sunday *Times*"

Willow Springs: "Loon," "Winter Beginning with *The Jerry Springer Show*"

"Blood" was reprinted in *Like Thunder: Poets Respond to Violence in America*
(University of Iowa) and *Are You Experienced: Baby Boom Poets at Midlife* (University
of Iowa). Section 3 of "Commotions" *appeared in New Poets of the Millennium*
(Godine). "Frost's Last Lecture: A Tape: His Audience" was reprinted in *Strongly
Spent: Fifty Years of Poetry* (Shenandoah) and *Poems on Robert Frost* (University of
Iowa). "Winter Beginning with *The Jerry Springer Show*" was reprinted in *Mantho-
logy* (University of Iowa) and *Under the Rock Umbrella* (Mercer University Press).

Thanks to Western Michigan University for its generous assistance.

I'd like to thank David Wojahn, Mary Ruefle, Beckian Fritz Goldberg, Alane Roll-
ings, and Jamie D'Agostino for their help and encouragement. Special thanks to
Nancy Eimers.

AVENUE OF VANISHING

Pretty soon they'll hear the suitcase of my heart,
then they'll open it and
                    put in the clouds
and the hard stars.

But for now my future was a hospital,
                    neither clouds nor stars,
nor day nor night.
Nurses were there and were not,

some black moon cast these white shadows.

It was an absolute hubbub
                    of a disaster,
old-fangled monitors and rickety metal saplings

bustling about with wheels for roots.

What must once have seemed forever
                    buoyed up and out—

the past must have loved me, though,
                    reluctant to hand me over.
And there was a father waiting outside
as they did back then.

The streets were astonishingly pacific.

Even the garbagemen had not yet woken,
                    no racing forms to sweep up yet,
no AK-SAR-BEN, no backwards Nebraska.

Nothing but wait, and the city asleep,
                    to my credit I was quick—

someone has jimmied the day open—
the inside is all bawl for all we know.

It was raining all the rain in Omaha,

umbrellas popping open,

whether I can prove it or not.

Wrapped up in cord and afterbirth,
I was a howl and an ugly beginner

and we still had to go outside.

PART

ONE

○

Infinity

It only wanted to say everything at once,
it would pull the very moment out of reach,
it blessed the muskrat among rusted reeds
gliding ahead of the shimmering geese and goslings—
it was in how their caliper wakes broadened out,
how the pond then zippered shut, in all that surface,
in all the glittering rosaries of dirt road potholes,
inside our ecstasy, even inside our withholding,
leaning into every dawn as if to part a frugal red sea—
it looked for itself in our famished countenance,
it was a mirror dreaming only of a hall of mirrors,
it was inside my voice and it was inside its echo,
in the dread of night and the dread of not-night,
in a big wind for an hour, then in the bigger calm,
in the hammock where all ghosts together lie,
whole months, years thundering all around it,
it was the same idea as always, so discerning,
knowing just when it was its time again to be,
when to tell the entire world what the world already knew
of the crimson nuclear reactors of our roses.
That's what infinity did, contain and threaten,
until friends complied by going one by one
to resurface obligingly in memories, and it sometimes still feels
we left them at our leisure, that such choice was good
so long as a larger choice seemed to succeed it,

nor could gazing bereave us of common sense,
nor would all plenty and foison fall into penury,
nor would shame forever drop its heavy head.
Infinity felt like life, and it said so, and waited.
It even spelled our autumnal names in solid gold
leaves that an inexhaustible supply of wind
tossed for such pleasure as we had said and said
until it transformed into the profound conviction
that the right track was lost—imagine—forever,
it turned our tears into pebbles that can't seep away,
that can't fly away, that we don't dare to pronounce,
yet it seemed concocted out of a clear beautiful sky,
yet it peeped out the woodshed and drank from the gutter spout,
yet it wrestled with itself and sank in eager mud
that presently it might be outwardly known
along with all the other creatures that perish,
heartbreaking idea among many heartbreaking ideas.

ALL MOON

We can't make it cry for us,
it's too old, it has its own
gravestones to revolve around.

It shines far outside itself
like a cry up from a well,
but it can't think to ask for help,

heaping obedient waves
over rocks, into tide pools,
its livelong, breaking task—

it won't stay long for us,
it can't stop our lunacy,
it's paralyzed, it's always news,

it looks so incidental,
erased by a cirrus scarf,
remote in its indifference,

all the nights we've stared at it
don't move it an inch closer,
it isn't about our gaze,

all its disappearing acts,
all its reappearing acts
we can't get out of our head

as if there were nothing but
time to look up and so what
if we are afraid of death,

yes it could be blown away
we think by a final breath—

ALL-AMERICAN

(first-grade class photo)

How shiny his tow hair, like car lights, shiny buttons,
how clean the teeth, how white the cardigan,
blue the eyes that might not recognize me
enough to pity what childhood has sired and deserted,

the large hands his slipped on like living gloves,
the hull his little ribs forgot their littleness for,
the mists of consciousness that enveloped him,
the heart that learned to race, or skip a beat—

a little red white and blue all-American emblem
sewed to his sweater as if to shield him
or make him take the shield—how loved he was,
this shiny grade-school photo, all the kids

(like the wisecracking stars of *Hollywood Squares*)
lined up one moment, sat in the same chair,
for backdrop the map turned round (like missing children
on milk cartons, or like windows in *Rear Window*),

flashed in the light (there is no other light)
we're all well on the other side of now:
there where all our longing was to be older
whatever outlasts that flash, was just a puff,

the school windows we looked out for the view,
the view we were of ourselves in the photos
embarrassed before our singular natures,
our faces all agreeability,

blank as buttons, or boutonnieres still boxed—
such quiet as outlasts the popping sounds,
spontaneous and repetitious,
our crossing over ruled and squared enough:

it was the sort of submission that asks for more.
Just a puff, the oak leaves from the school's one oak
hanging in noisy clumps for their lives by their lives,
just a puff our first grade, Class of Not So Quick,

Class of Noisemakers spastic most of the time,
turning, topsy-turvy with gesticulation,
never blowing away (although we did),
watching that oak strip all year, never seeing enough,

Oak of Deciduous Distinctions, each leaf hanging
to its life without the slightest knowledge
sunlight was on it that spectacular way
that sunlight has of being little weight,

our families out of the picture, we spectacularly lit
by some half-seen, half-felt embarrassment
before our very own accepting natures,
we memories that fidgeted without moving much,

disciplined by light that doesn't think or read,
light that sits down anywhere it pleases
without a chair or school desk, or permission slip,
each smile holding up a WELCOME mat,

yet another one-time chosen generation,
each portrait the size of an uncanceled four-cent stamp—
unused, untraveled—pupils, flash-lit pupils—
remaining seated for all that any light is worth,

for all that any life reveals—the view we were—
we singularities lined up for our turn,
even the precocious troublemakers fallen in line—
faces white as petals, white as surrender flags,

white as sharks, as teeth, white slowed to glacial,
white as surprise in the face of someone just shot
who remembers to breathe and live, and lives, or doesn't. . . .
Americans, we were family members first

inside the family car or the family restaurant,
home in the family room, watching family TV:
inside the family we were the only "we";
at school we were a slightly different "we."

Our baby booming smiles must have shot forth
too unexceptionally to have marred our future
staring like possibility from the ruled windows
of America baring its inner lives—

even if there is no singular consciousness—
I can bring back maybe every other name,
I can believe this much of our shared past,
I can believe this much of our past can't touch us to hurt us,

I can see that little all-American emblem
my mother sewed to my fleece-white cardigan,
I can affirm a "we," a generation
without a purpose yet except to beam.

GEGENSCHEIN: 1959

It'd take an Etch A Sketch to get down those spindly parking lot
trees guy-wired to islands of greenery,
it'd take an aperceptual bulldozer to pave

that aboriginal parking lot of happy cars,
black sheepfold almost precognitive,
cars spanking clean as beautiful, prizewinning babies—

style all came down to these cars,
sheer wishfulness, all contour.
It'd take a child Leviathan to conceive such justly curving fins.

Or the two sons singing *Nixon Nixon he's my man,*
let's throw Kennedy in the frying pan—
sky's powder-blue tuxedo lapel pinned

with pink carnations of big cumulus clouds,
big make-believe,
civility in the manner of a few loose primary-family crowds,

and happiness, who can turn it away?
A five-year-old species of happiness,
watching the sun poke through, a sudden nipple,

another nipple just above a steeple
earliest memory's earnest milk money.
Two oranges, one blood, one mock,

mother all style and all guileless and all
fitted in black pumps and father all Saturday sport-jacket style
it'd take a mnemonist to reckon with

in the last century of metrical parking meters.
1959—all years, all numbers scanned,
every numbered dot the crayon children connected,

numbered stars of coloring books, their numbered constellations,
numbers stenciled on the jumpsuits of our criminals—
and nobody's license plates had their personalized ego ideals yet.

A five-year-old was watching the leaves of the few
parking lot silver maples turn up their undersides
all submissively at once, so summer school–like,

each with the brute insistence of a pike.
Against such sparse spirited machinery
human effort does not seem naive yet,

one billion Barbie dolls do not yet repel us,
the promulgation of the human image
has not yet reached its current critical mass,

the books about names wronging things have not
yet found their way into any circulation,
circumspect, circumstantial style not yet called to fuss

over the depressing separation of the world of the dead
from the world
of the living.

It can come undone in a moment.
It is always a moment style
goes looking for to marry the many eternities,

coming out of the mall always to the one
twice-sunny moment dead and alive again,
food for thought, food for body, floor mats for the car:

more funereal black cars then than now, each a night-polished jackboot—
Rambler, Chrysler, Studebaker, Ford.
No style of talk, parental or childlike, had a word

for this second sun above Arcadia,
two suns, two expert liars, two towheaded blinding radia,
ninety degrees, eye rhymes, simulacra, second sun *O what am I*

wonder's postnatal outrage must have wondered—
the five-year-old answer crossing with his brother and parents
over the freshly summer-tarred gullet

of asphalt, disappearing into a Chrysler bullet,
honesty no excuse for metrical cudgel work.
Honestly, no name comes up from the murk—

across such sloughs of happiness we must have walked the Jesus walk,
we must have talked the parent talk and the child talk,
two suns, two parents, two madras-shirted sons:

a hundred times or so each day we died.
Some breeze since gotten doubled up inside. . . .
But two suns in only this one moment,

small breeze lifting up each silver leaf
like a nurse might the intravenous-needled hand of a preemie—
even when the rainless breeze picks up

and the spirited machinery of our dual-headlighted single-carbureted
Chrysler resurrects mechanical hiccups,
the four of us wedged in the front seat,

used car gnashing homeward like one tooth,
the otherness of other shoppers
etch-a-sketched, erased by the same quickening style

in memory's refracted mirage-oasis,
shoppers standing straight as altar-boy candle flames
in actual, obdurate sunshine

and not-fake not-real sunshine.
Four of us wondering what *is* that that bears down twice on little familiar travels
and the least of us in age and in this language

wondering right now why is there now only style
that one moment of one day be monumental, beautiful,
green-stamp baseball parks irredeemable

even if the fly balls are retrievable.
Impossible,
redoubtable double celestial sunburst peacefulness

without a body bag, or a name tag for a coroner.
This arcadian apocalypse not yet died down
to middle world and recall's muddled midlife,

embers of streetlights on lazy summer nights—
parking-lot buggy babies doing what babies do,
crying like burst carotids,

each fallen leaf met by the neatly folded
monogrammed jacket of a shadow from prep school,
each correspondence rich in the instant as we were,

we four breathers together in all weather,
we prayers taking on the sight of others,
these sights outlasting all the fathers and mothers,

mothers and fathers, and daughters, and uniformed sons
out on the farthest reaches of chemical diamonds slurping kamikazes,
orange mixed with grape—

just as in the eastern skies—
Gary, Indiana–smog sifting spectacularly down.
Petroglyphic tire treads, lick and fawn the highway's double line . . .

sun, twice over dead or alive, please please us, pretty please, shine.

The Managerial Sublime

(Jane Addams Line)

But there is Wolf Lake and people on pebbly causeways
casting real parti-colored lines for real mercurial fish,
and just past where the Falstaff plant used to be with its giant granaries
painted up as a six-pack for some titanic cheap-buzz thirst,
there's a dead blue strip of lake, like a cobalt razor strop
upon which no Sunday strollers promenade, and Hammond streets
are empty as the inside of a rose in a burning photo of a rose,
empty as the Empress Casino boat and the empty spinning wheels,
as if there were not always enough steam to distraction
to create a people without a pinch of inwardness.
Is it the nature of the sublime to unpeople a Sunday dawn?
The sublime sees one steel tanker pass through the steel zigzag
braces of a pylon crewed by people the sublime has never been or seen.
This absence of ourselves to each other must have been thought up.
But what thought contrives the sycamore and sumac
bent by wind, kowtowing goodbye and motion sick,
or busted limestone blocks the size of bank vaults for a shoreline
or Coke Express boxcars filled with sheet-metal scraps compressed to lyric
    contortion,
what thought made the smokestacks billow cauliflower florets
while train tracks cross and recross like the paths of drunks,
there being no single paths in a world this interdisciplinary—
only long solemn shuntings to explain, apropos of nothing,
contrariety's compacted sheet metal in flatbeds and gondolas.
None of the landscape is moving, all of it is waiting to move

past the Trump Hotel, its filet-mignon-pink casino boat
docked like a brave vibration each way free, secured, fulfilled—empty.
Internalized description arranges each and every *nature morte*.
But this is too close to Pavese's description of *The Iliad*,
every locus umbilically connected—productivity mirroring productivity—
to some steel womb of a steel mother with a hundred steel arms to hug,
suspension bridges from one refinery to the next, tollbooth houses atop them,
where trolls with sulfur breath and steel-wool hair perpetuate
the annihilation of anything that stirs with a face,
suspension bridges loaded with steel cottages for gear work,
steelyards almost all desuetude, the glory days long gone.
Inside the heart of a factory so old its shadows are rusted,
the sublime could cosset steel lambs lapping up steel blood let from a steel
    gash,
their inhuman eyes fixed upon the inhuman managerial heart,
their inhuman paschal smiles lowered to inhuman blood—
inhuman automatons breathing in the secondhand smoke of smelters—
far from hell and where if we cry we drown out other cries
and if we do not cry we come to where the phantoms live,
and the stench goes to bed with the stench, as nature only puts us out,
it reproduces too slowly, it dies its deaths too slowly
on this Sabbath when only one businessman on a cell phone
leans into the face of another businessman on a cell phone,
and a mother's child attaches to glass like a postage stamp,
his hands when she finally peels him off leaving specters of sweat that grasp at
    what goes,
that are the ghost of a grasp, the eidos of a preference for the past—
a long stretch of lily pad ponds and sycamores and oaks,
the dead rushes and the living energies they catalogue,
miles of gondolas stretching empty across sand stretches,
uninhabited steelworks, uninhabited lakeshores,
uninhabited streets of the occasional trailer parks,
us slowing down to a steel sigh, to stop at Michigan City,
a Mennonite woman getting on with Pullman luggage,
trees gawking over steel-wire fences in sedated idiocy

while the concrete spindles of two nuclear reactors
rise above a playground's vacated Potemkin village of plastic toy houses—
look how they shine bright, this very day that everything outside the head is
reproduces almost nothing but the wheels of spinning light.
I gouge everything into the spiral-bound book of delight
like the sap of Charles Sheeler, his *Architectural Cadences*—
squat salt-lick powerhouses that duplicate themselves
unto the softening airborne versions of sheer pleasance,
with factory clouds like parade streamers streaming upwards from heaven
    itself,
pushing to the next deadening level of the sublime,
coke ovens, steel cutters, dynamos, slag buggies,
forms existing on their own terms, the utilitarian dispositions:
the vast mechanism has its own life for conquest and future missionary work,
the chimney and the smoke that spews from it are equally fastidious,
totems of steel trelliswork cranes hoist archangelic pulleys,
porcelain insulators rosary-beaded all the way to the welkin
and not anything but the backs of people to walk into landscape
as impersonal units that reinforce the overall design
and emphasize the grandeurs and the atmospheric verities,
even the ghosts of factories in Benton Harbor closed for Sunday,
Saint Joseph's lazy curvilinear streets for brand-new housing pods,
with not one corporeal crow in these bare saplings,
only stacks both great and small in celebration of a blue haze of heaven
where even our brute industry is now antiquated
by gravity-free, circuit-woven silicon and Mylar.
The white pines were "mined," the factory rats largely exterminated—
if this is Sunday in truth this must be the rapture.
Only it seems no one was even supposed to live.
That was the idea of Corbusier's house, "a machine for living"—
a miniature factory for the production of comfort—
of creating agoraphobic voids belted by "Chinese walls,"
of superhighway billboards principled on the "less is a bore" theory,
streets lined with cars emptied of Sunday drivers, our train
heaving with the basic suburban asexual starts and stops.

There's not many of us to despise on this Sunday morning train,
shout away all creation and no one would look up,
at best momentum's a memory, at worst a ghost—
locked in the heart's blast furnace where we needed it the most—
noon's door somehow pushing back all the light,
daytime, daybreak, light of day, light of dawn,
light from the suffix of *naked*, to shine, be white,
light with its human syllables adrift and far apart.

The World Below

this litel spot of erthe
—CHAUCER

Let the extraterrestrials look down upon our cities sprung from murder,
and our buses stalled beneath starlight, and still decide to land,
step out from their steel husks under the shaken trees,
stare up at a stalk of red light softly clicking green,
kneel with their helmets off, breathe in the smog, grasp at a tendril of car
   exhaust.
Stepping over a plot of irises braying their pollinated sighs,
scraping into an agar dish the rust off the grotesque claw of a garden rake,
antennae teetering toward the steam rising from the dewy yards,
tuning in each grassblade's brutally innocent aspirations,
muttering logarithmically, shaking thick-veined heads, eyes shrunk to
   inhospitable pinholes,
pondering why downstreet, in a Plexiglas cubicle, a ringing goes unanswered,
apparitional in their curiosity, ancient themselves in their infinitely rational
   natures,
as they towel their own inscrutable fingerprints off
every last material clue of who we think we are and why,
as they gaze skyward at the corpselight of their own sun, let them feel
instant and tranquil and bereaved in our alien night.

GODS AND GODDESSES

Barely morning when a red air balloon flying over our house awoke us with the hiss of propane and for one fantastic moment its big bloody teardrop blocked the sky in our window while up above the tree line heavenly voices we could hear from bed called down to earth or went on talking in a flying picnic basket whisked away from us before we could jump out of bed and run outside and call back up and wave goodbye.

By a Railroad Crossing

One day our signatures will ascend from our wills
with all the rubbish of our little dusks.

We'll give up on redemption, for the time will have passed
for waiting around like abuse for angels to board us.

That instant after language and solitude
a page of the phone book will blow away, with a few more.

And a last human voice will argue
the unconditional terms of perpetual sadness.

The white face of the earth, streetlight off snow.
One street, one train, one stoplight to go green.

This shall be the last night of our very first lives,
and what this means shall pass like empty berths.

PART

TWO

○

Ease

(the Yakima River)

It is oblivious to be sure but it is not oblivion,
it tugs at every branch, fallen, stuck, black, valedictory,
the course that confines it it wears down to talus,
yet there are trees free of its course full of starlings,
darting parabolas over the water and back,
tumultuous muscles in the currento, transparent difficulties,
unseen disappearances, pitch pine glinting in noonlight.
And we all want to get by, me, her, our two friends,
their singular, overappreciative, overappreciated kid—
their chubby kid, their sweet innocent kid tugs at the heart—.
And though our childlessness tugs at the heart too,
though our envy of their child and their envy of our childlessness
are best left unspoken, though some inner weather is all blather,
though the best white water is upstream, we pick downstream,
we take our time, we stall out in the quiet spots
so we can feel the ease and Judy can send the sinuous signature of a fly line
out to where water riffles just enough for trout—
it is like reading, this one raft floating downstream—
it is like when I read and am most taken up by what I read
and I forget my consciousness of why I am reading—
familial, marital tensions all concord—motley crew—
someone points and before I have the time to recall who
an insane osprey plumbs a dead-line vertical drop, and dives,
and surfaces with a trout and flaps away like a gigantic chimney ash.
One of its feathers, shed to drift, and be a souvenir,

seems somehow as steadfast and heavy as the stones beneath it in the stream.
I know precisely why this obvious lingering should be so.
All this here-and-elsewhere, all this lightweight out-of-reach quintessence.
I know change can't let go and I also know what infinity is.
Our digressing raft, all air, beaches in a crook in the bank,
we'll deflate it and push it into the back of a pickup half rust,
and all that is left will be narrative, though that is a lot to be left,
for that leaves us to immerse ourselves before narrative passes,
us swimming above bum spider threads and lost fishing lines,
us with burning noses and toes to cool, us to shun the flies,
then leave the water where its ease is enfolding, folding, old,
married with child, child, childless, ease is taking leave of all our senses.

Commotions

1

Zennor Crows, Cornwall

Row by row is how fields gash.
They throw some crows into a gust,
pinched little show.

Mud or muck can't think up one last crow.
But each dawn crows boomerang back.
On the roof of a piggery in ruin

they alight with donnish formality,
abstractly watching an empty truck
the turnip pickers parked.

Puddles are marooned in rutted tracks.
The crows look indivisibly stuck
even as their numbers multiply,

shining like church shoes,
strict rows on phone wires:
far too like a metaphor

all the light's gone from.
Eyeing baby-wrinkled
Aladdin's-lamp turnips

hacked, massacred, heaped in a truck,
ransacked, sacked, tied up.
More pick some carcass

naked even of nakedness.
Language, don't cry.
Flesh blows away. Crows blow away,

scavengery without malice.
The stubborn fact, stripped, whistles.
Piggeries blow away—

the Zennor church will blow away.
We and the crows belong
and the turbulence carries.

2

Out of Love

Out of love we fall ten times a day.
Out of the marrow, out of luck,
out back into distractions and joys we rip off from prey,

like yanking a claw off a lobster,
then putting it and the tail and the little motile feet
back down on the plate

and looking up from it with the mug of a mobster—
big baby boy with his bib tied on—
just before the spray of bullets

sends the waiter and busboys ducking for cover—
but nothing goes wrong or cinematic yet,
the premonitions have not yet invented regret—

we create
this moment that leaves the spectacle of shipwrecks out,
pull out the egg-white chocolate flesh, and eat, and lick.

Love is not love unless love momently slaps
down a credit card, and saunters ahead or behind the other in this
    Bar Harbor agora
of fake lobster traps and a restaurant built to look like a lobster trap—

unless the first room in a lobster trap—
the kitchen—leads to the bedroom.
Under the counter, lobster clocks and lobster playing cards.

If love is a stainless steel trap,
two of us are caught in it,
and the good question of the strange young April light

travels lighter and lighter at the bottom of the ocean,
drifts with the silver seabed silt through fishing net.
We pass by yachts in a boatyard girdled with concertina wire

turned into strings of stars by spring dew.
You have the speechless, headlight-silvered profile
of the Indian on the buffalo nickel.

Inside your face your lovely parents appear
at the end of their lives eating dinner
out of their absolutely poignant love.

Wet asphalt the color of a gun barrel.
Rain pings on the hood.
Tires ahead of us slash through it sending up broken strings of pearls.

As if from no distance at all,
rain continues to fall.
It is a message seen through enough

to drive back to the bedroom all over again,
it is a prelude to an afterlife.
Futuristic see-through lobster dormitories,

the sun that boiled pink color,
slate bobtail gravestones lifting their names in last little light, huge little light.
Whole worlds disappear each night

and the small sad lies stand looking out of us both—
out of your or my peremptory joys,
out of your or my wan resentments,

remembered face on a remembered window—
your glee's reflection today at L'Étoile de Mer's window.
The daily catch today is mackerel,

gangrene-green, emulsion-silver, jail-cell striped,
your face caught with the fish on the other side of the glass,
the colorful finale, gill slits, wan smiles on crushed ice,

another and another and another.
Out of the father and the mother—
waves grind to flatliners on granite shelves,

cresting to forms seen partly through,
annihilated as without annihilation
love really would disappear—

out of love the future doesn't care
to kiss or tell, won't take us in,
it has no head for the distances called the soul,

sea shingled in crooked glimmers
out of rhapsody and rant,
out of love evolving out of lack,

sails teetering on the threshold. . . .

Defining Style: Nova Scotia Snapshot Lying on the Sunday *Times*

This week's Saks ad again defines style as
supermodel unawareness, statuesque,
just the right sane slightly wanton fit,

pleasantries of irony, indifferent air.
Style starts with the stylet, then the stiletto,
then the stiletto heels and then

the slap in the face, the crumpling blonde,
earthsick flicks without a sprig of green,
people who think and fart percentages

not unlike the stink of the gunpowdered whale gun.
The prolongation of the ovary,
or the calyx that holds the bud, or this very pen

that writes the granite steps that lead from one
beshitted field to another in the old country
till the landrobbed Scots took to the new country.

And the landlord highlanders following these,
with the halibut bat the salts would call "the priest,"
with the awl, the awled, the awed

journeying souls, the boring arrogant male,
the bored, arrogating female,
you, me, Nova Scotia snapshot,

the open moment that poured through its porthole
aperture, a nautical museum,
all the years the animal got flensed,

foghorn barely plowing its way through
to all the aspects you are, posed there,
your hand stopwatched in a modest stylish wave,

real because I choose to call you real,
real regardless of the style I choose,
real in a nave of two sperm whale ribs,

the rest of the whale fallen out of fashion,
out of matter itself for that matter,
out of anything we'd call continual.

4
Fear in Style

A box of barbed hooks looks like a printer's box
of Russian letters unstrung from their epic sentences.
You write our names out with them,
then back away—
if love's commotions can never be spelled out,
if the soul is the distance between the two of us
and doesn't read or talk and won't take us in
for this evening or the rest of our lives,
then its elegances decline into the daily awkwardnesses,
who stand evoking each other at each other,
lurking above some hooks like two time-dial shark fins,
our steely names spelled out by hooks.
The names say the hook evolved from a lost tooth,
the styles from the hook, style from the style.
We're two blunt oars in this nautical museum,
Nova Scotia, and the clarifying aperture opens
to our fury and rue and psychology and fire
and all the aspects of the woman you are.
Your mouth clenches against its given name.

Your mouth is closed but eyes and face stay open,
I think they have no choice that they are.
Your human eyes upon the human ocean,
your human smile lowered to a slow blue pilot-light burn,
nothing goes wrong yet,
so what is this love I wish to throw a rope to—
whose eye is this in the hook love wishes to thread—
the boats are rocking with their gilded names,
the names rock, too, the names shall grasp at a straw.

5

Penwith Crows

Crows squint into dusk the boatlights outlast
and the thousand small sad lies stand looking
out of the private dark of the body,
out of rant and rhapsody and joy,
out of love and out of the father's boy
and his mother's hurt magic and her rich cares
all blown somewhere across moon's toothless light,
heartsick triumphs, refined bad moods,
harrowings, misgivings, the dead holding their ears,
tantrums, scorn metastasized to rage,
until the night is like a stroll in death
and such boatlights should almost be past breath,
outlasting dusk, hanging sometimes to thought,
crawling past all of the tactical ecstasies.

Sotto Voce

All our life we've heard and heard and heard
about silence while the inextinguishable stars
are many silences, many perforations—
each star nosing through like a lazy mole
all last night—the townie bars now closed
while a slow wind teases the locust trees out of their silences
and the slow silent light on the street the leaves shuffle
is as my bright thoughts of night. These thoughts
silence. As I was silent most of the night.
I think of night all day until I get it right,
while a few bird cheeps flake off the shingles.
Hum of a tar mixer—grind of a road grader—
before our species vanishes it must widen
the road downtown, for beautification is ugly—
some silent protester placed these small white crosses
at the shorn trunks of the maples and black oaks—
they've torn up the living street, bare dirt
where asphalt once was, a few tree stubs
with silent wooden rings like wedding rings
widening out to the reaches of oblivion
without which there would be no room for us,
no room anyway—it's all one sound track—
whoosh of a UPS truck, locust leaves that temporize,
changing their positions like politicians.
And there is silence as of a silencer too,
couple of June bug husks wedged in the front door screen,
uninhabited bullets—and my soul stalls,

to silence, mine, yours, ours, silence of our pencils—
teethed and sharpened, lead dust scattered to the stars,
stacks of silent fine stock paper watermarks,
blank sheet with a technoluminescent lull
just like that of house lights mirrored in puddles—
gathered rain, rain that sent silent neighbors
inside, their voices shred into happy,
unremembering confetti, and the old
silent shoe of the moon doesn't have a tongue.
There are craters pocking that silence, that far up
silence is almost some ultimate language
of circumference, the silence around the moon
conversing with the silence of the moon,
where Kewpie doll astronauts bagged the lunar rocks
and the unremembering footprints still look
back on us with their crumbled, faraway stares.
Looking back on earth that has been unearthed,
Main Street flensed of half its asphalt—it's one way now—
my barrens or your wasteland, the daily traffic
is easier to cross now, I wish I could disclose
for you everything positive about such silence
without turning my own silence inside out
or disrespecting the cat's silent supercell of sleep
or the dust on the sill from the turned up road
or my turned off stupefied Fender practice amp.
The silences of the dinosaur are we, we
are silent dust watching more silent dust settle.
Silence of a shadow government, such
silence that as some last answer says behaves
"as though it had the right to more," silent faces,
each dawn's commuters—or do they lip-sync the silence—
and the soul stalls, and the stalling has no name.
Blown pinnate locust leaves, branches creaking all day,
by night gone still as spines—these silences
so easily confused with the silence of the snuffed

candle, the sudden end, fell destruction—
the lie of death we keep rehearsing so we can sleep
the complete unsurpise of sleep—unshattered halos,
streetlights that trail off to no end of ellipses . . .
the silent embolus in the brain's right hemisphere,
this silent morning with a helicopter in it—
a grub with wings, a thought that isn't mine—
our neighbor trying and failing to start his mower—
bless some failures, bless some silences,
bless that we've had our dead and that it was an honor
to fear our own lives in their lapsing silences,
enough that such blunt distinctions aren't over.
Is this day-wind your or my sleeplessness:
which of us can speak it? These silences
play tricks on the eyes and now I see us
a million silences away, we have a sea view
along the Ligurian coast, lake slubbed with boats,
then a silent barge cutting across the molten lead road
across the sea the setting sun has paved,
fishing boats sounding out just like didgeridoos.
In memory the noisiest boat is a silence.
That was a long time ago, that gift of noise.
That gift opened up to implausibly silent
apartments on implausibly noisy streets,
to sounds that are neither day nor night.
Then, now, later, some momentous moment,
silent clothes on our clothesline now below
glass window pane a good hundred years old,
wavery, shot through with air bubbles—
the silence of these is older than we are.

Loon

And spring and then the child on its back.

Human love is different. It is an indoors.
A fire collapses, smoke spirals heavenwards—

And two shapes of sleep scarcely breathe.

The windows are stunned to transparency.
You look out one for something besides us.

Something outside where first drops of rain—
Soon they must stop—start falling now.

These last few days of it have been total losers
I say and it's true enough and false enough

To be a helpless child of a thing to say.
Love gets over us, whole seasons pass.

And fall's unused boats like upturned ears.
And winter and more of anything but that.

We sense the lack of future in ourselves.

The sudden sun goes down because it does,
Suddenly it does, memory is our wilderness.

It returns without a sound, that sane cry.

A Few of the Many Numbered Birds
of the State of Oaxaca

1

I sat next to a crow on a bus. We tried to talk, unsuccessfully, about the oldest tree in the world, in El Tule, then he went back to sleep. Just once he roused, to take off his straw cowboy hat and spit out the bus window, almost hitting a policeman on the shoulder.

2

Black seraphs rising from roadkill.

3

Cassiques, turistas, jays, trogons, parakeets, parrots, *curaçÕes,* beer-bottle quetzalcoatls.

4

American cardinals in cages rising from the back of a bird hawker, a twelve-feet-high mobile ziggurat.

5

All the bad news of another day doesn't stop. Nor does it stop the Mercado's stalls from opening, the knife grinder from sending sparks from the edge of the blade where no edge is. Nor does it stop him from staring through us to the black magic stall where a string of dried hummingbirds and a string of dried toucans with shipwrecked canoes for beaks are twisting like magnetic needles towards the arctic afterlife called Polaroid.

6

Turkeys are everywhere. Turkeys in wheelbarrows, turkeys tucked under the arms of Zapotec mothers, turkeys in baby prams, turkeys in shopping bags. But only this one in the butcher shop, the Corazón de Jesús, is tucked into itself, its bookmark beak buried in down, its feet twined, trying to get up before the old new world throws the mantle of starlight over its shoulder and brings down the cleaver.

7

Here in church is a sad sparrow named Christ, crimson velvet shorts, grayed flesh, stigmata, matted black tresses, lying on his plucked breast, a languishing centerfold. Erotica: behind glass. A glass case, a glass coffin: a glass barque. And another sparrow, another Christ, standing off to the side. This one holds a cane sideways, with photos of dead children safety-pinned to the hem of his crimson robe. His tresses came from a wig shop, too. He has a long face from presiding over the sorrow of worship.

8

The little yellow birds in the scrub, flying fruit, are screaming as if they chose to be screaming, perhaps that's joy.

9

The grackle at a Mary shrine has yellow eyes, a black rudder, and skintight feathered legs. Claws spurred, it hops around with its head bent toward the ground with the posture of one of the early dinosaurs, the ones with grandmotherly, effeminate forearms. Only it comports itself like a sleek businessman right out of business school.

10

The rooster that calls near dusk must have the apocalypse backwards.

11

The green jays in their men's pickups coming to market are smiling just like us. In the puddles of their green mantillas, they convince me that the earth has ended before. They seem older than the earth, greener than the earth, earthier. The part of them that isn't smiling is a deep rattle.

12

Next to the Corazón de Jesús is a cathedral the color of a cattle egret. By night every pigeon in the dusty streets is tucked away between the sandstone saints.

13

Then outside is dark again as the inside of this cathedral. Where wall meets ceiling, before the celestial icons begin, mirrors are facing downward—if you position yourself correctly you can see yourself, wingless but looking downward at yourself, puzzled at gravity.

14

The streetlights would be going off soon on streets that finally existed. Soon, the living lights called canaries. Soon, the green jays that seem greener than the earth. Soon, a crippled laughing gull to hop on one leg to all this good news. Soon, the thieving frigate birds to replace the fat-cat stars over the bay. And there would be more birdcalls like skeleton keys in rusted locks, birdcalls that scraped like a fire ladder of a burning building, birdcalls that presuppose birds as loneliness presupposes memory and love presupposes even more memory, birdcalls like unoiled hinges of the doors that close behind us. One bird actually crying like one of those doll babies you press to make cry. The silence had to break long before you could know it. Birdcalls making that metallic sound that drops of water do when pulled off the eaves, into the uncontainable.

Study of the Resurrection

"JESUS IS COMING; LOOK BUSY"
—A BUMPER STICKER

It is tempting to imagine the imperial surgeon's hands raising living gloves of
    blood.
It is tempting to wish to dissect the anatomist himself,
the body of Vesalius, say, beginning with the eye
which cannot otherwise imagine itself to see itself
—and pass through the origin of the superior oblique
to the articulated skeletons of these Amsterdam plane trees
assuming the postures of gibbeted breadstealers,
this moment lowering its eyes below understanding.
Past the naked booths with the naked ones
go nervous truculent throngs, red-light district inanely antique,
past somebody's daughter drawing a tram ticket
tattooed with ocher and black and indigo numbers
so plainspokenly along such lips as needn't speak
that the worst for her must be unbelievable.
So many beautiful kindnesses and so many horrible wants of kindness
and such healthy desire and such unhealthy desires—
not as when desire fantasizes and sleeves again, again,
her bones in flesh, and as pebbles in a stream her every cleft again shows—
though this is insipid enough—but as when some young girl
sits in a box all day zoned out peeling a Heineken label
and it is scarcely possible to understand the living pictures,
the evenings we hope one day to find even the first word for,
the Velvet Canal where the middle class was practically born,

this city of tolerance, sex slaves, kept art, and merciful death,
the onetime surreptitious Catholic Amstelkring,
the Frank family's door leading to the stairs to the mirror that reflected one
    oak
still trying to strip all winter as if we would never see enough,
the trolleys that are moving accordions opening to new streets,
new sights to love past temptation of death, past the resurrection,
a few clumps of bottommost leaves by a door thrown open to a strobe—
how each articulated snowflake seems to want itself again and again in
    writing,
in black-and-white, putting on the dark and then the light,
every church brick pulled from the fire then from the forge,
every window of every city staring through everything,
inside or outside everybody alive, right there in front of us.

Neither Paradise nor Below, nor Up nor Down

The one-legged beggars in Rome are like the Signorelli figures on the west wall in this cathedral in Orvieto. The figures pulling themselves, and each other, limb by limb, out of and up from flesh-colored ground.

This cathedral, striped horizontally with different colored granite, the dull pink and dull gray of well-washed prisoner clothes,

later will be the color of translucence, then, long after human history, a color all hollow, then the color of space as far as the night can see.

Just last night I dreamed there were escalators in the cathedral, and madonna-like figures like unearthed terra-cotta warriors posted in corners of sensory neglect, and all the subways and the architraves and station islands and all holy location vacated by everything I ever was and am

but perspective. A dream wasn't a cathedral, and it wasn't the Rome Terminal, and it wasn't day or night.

Now the cathedral houses a piece of cloth that someone is said to have said he saw bleed, making imaginable Sight itself.

The newly resurrected are still there, struggling to free themselves in a cathedral light that looks

palpably like the light in the Rome subways as it drapes the one-legged beggars. Only these stay put for as long as they beg. One woman, at the end of her workday, covers up her stump and its imploring pucker. She rocks by her crutches to the escalators, rising, like all the others, in single file, there being no room to rise to daylight's last cries but one by one.

Spit

It all keeps coming from the mouth,
inexhaustible renewal of vocables
all getting over us, seasons passing
while cigarette boats plow the same blues up innocuously,
riding the easting of our listening
until their very irrepressible sound
flatlines with waves into formality.
These passing facts impoverish us,
signs that explain the genius of the place,
the photo of a near-extinct sand plover
nailed to a power pole like a Wanted poster.
Why the gulls are laughing never reaches shore
and happiness, who can argue with it:
one never knows if it is toying with one—
otherness can sound just like derision.
Though it could be despair, it could be
the most familiar unexceptional beings
cry survivably for the soon-to-perish,
laugh survivably for the soon-to-flourish
or simply mew or buzz as passing facts,
a cloud of gnats so easily seen through
their individuals might as well not exist.
The point of one perspective is that everything
sounds as though we try too hard to listen.
The only why of listening is to hold fast
not prematurely letting go, as lives must,
not punishing ourselves when we do let go

while beyond reach of even our spectacular souls
the sudden sun goes down because it did.
The more the past kept saying it didn't exist,
the more we believed its lie, until it didn't.
Books became instruments of forgetting,
even our languages, even the live ones,
even the one that currently rules the earth.
But not even this language can conceal itself,
it is as water that finds its own level,
it is as what will remain of our being,
heat rash of ruby lights upon the bay,
boats straggling in under every condition
before another dawn breaks into hesitation,
hesitation into dread, dread into our resting place,
into rest, the rest into rust, purple loosestrife,
the rest into a cat tail mauled by a red wing,
the rest that is the wonder it is to stare
at anything to keep it in sight but distant—
an inconclusiveness, both in the abstract
and in the shining gut. Like this fluttering leaf
bright on one side, blemished on the other.
It falls, once on the sand it recalls that falling.
Out of no end there unwinds a little wind.
And the leaf that recalls falling to the earth
looks up at the sky as if the sky were a tree.
And that leaf still keeps falling . . . skitters
a few lateral inches, among the sand crabs.
And the stars seem to come up out of a grave,
the mouth that it all comes up shining out of,
the mouth that from the very beginning lacks a face.
The surface falsely called the surface ruffles
like riches and fame were in it for it to do so—
any more imminence glitters on the surface,
any more immortality is of a passing nature.

PART

THREE

BLOOD

Sometimes blood looks for an opening,
any way to get out from under us and the knives.
Blood cuts into blood to look and its hands grasp blood.
My block is a corral of yellow crime-scene tape.
Twenty cop cars--
sometimes blood looks at blood for an explanation.
It turns out the whole block slept through a murder.
A social worker was stabbed by her psychotic charge
not two houses down, near the door of the Headstart school,
where the underprivileged play catch-up next door to the door to the School
    for the Disabled.
Both schools are underfunded, with all their school-day lives.
Call us childish, call us to our teachers:
a cop with a clipboard calls me over, to ask me what of blood I heard.
He knows in his blood better than to say it that way.
He puts it neutrally, may his heart feel adjudged by restraint,
may the differently abled be restrained for their own good,
and when I say *his* "heart" may I mean *mine* and may my mouth feel antique—
what he asks me is if I heard any cries—no, not even that, just . . . "anything."
Let's get this right.
Does a dying self make up a face as it goes, will any face do?
Right there on the concrete a bloodstain the children will pass, to touch it:
what's to touch once blood stops doing its cartwheels?
Someone has stepped out from under our thumbs and heels?
Can anyone ever make blood do anything? Can clouds be pushed around?
On and on till the questions are all open coffins.
Sleepy me, a cop, a schizo the state sent packing

and a dead do-gooder the papers will leach till her photo is a window after
    death.
By the windows of institutional ministration the cop
glances away from me at wheelchairs, spokes aglitter
like Ezekiel's chariot about to commence his convictions.
God cares that our families and homelands are slaughtered for being weak.
We are all victims, down to the butchers among us?
Weakness has strength, even if it hasn't killed us?
Coffins.
I drive by these windows each day, some strapped in headgear,
others who can be trusted to walk careen from wall to wall—
one always laughs with an "it's not funny" lodged in his laugh;
another always carries a Raggedy Ann doll with a sewed smile
and button eyes hanging by threads,
the stuffing coming out of it, affection has mauled it—
she holds tight what even oblivion gave up torturing,
clouds shining, her wheelchair passes me, a cop and our laws and our clue,
    blood;
its driver squints smiling into a happiness that is its own skewed warding of
    us off,
her wheelchair shines—O steel throne—a fool might even believe
she would wish to reign over our disabling kingdom.

54

Winter Beginning with *The Jerry Springer Show*

What we run towards on our treadmills is four TVs,
        channeled today and every day towards judgment.
           Why we have to run
is obesity, bad backs, mental ague,

low self-esteem, the usual or unusual daily
        aches and pains.
           Who we are
is running with everyone, running on adrenaline toward

adrenaline—. The walls are mirrors, the mirrors
        reflect us,
           we surround
ourselves, all hopeful bodily subtraction,

all of us running everywhere at once,
        nowhere is arrival,
           all of us unspeakingly
watching four TVs convey our ministries,

our trials of taste by millions—
        cuckolds, sad underaged mothers, giddy transsexuals.
           It's Christmas, almost.
Almost it is time

to resume the body's foibles, the paunch,
        the varicose
                insinuations of
the future,

flabby thighs, slack pecs,
        crippling differences.
                Everybody runs toward everybody's story
and smiles or grunts towards a trial that nobody wants—

2

the world outside nobody wants because want kills us—
        twilight crawling slowly with its rutting traffic,
            moon peering
from a tight cloud,

streets the snow has wished into a fairy tale,
        VAC SHACK,

            RAINTREE MUFFLERS
the VELVET TOUCH, the door of which keeps opening

like the eye of some roadkill,
        every revelation
        a veil,
so many sad contraptions, so many blue movies,

so many chains and dildoes, whips and handcuffs
        without a worldly care,
            the object-silence
of love dolls with those awful open mouths—

I click the sound off,
        winter outside keeps secret less and less,
                the snow belongs to everybody,
the streets snow wishes into a fairy tale belong to everybody.

The Klan now celebrating Christmas on four TVs,
        we run in judgment
                toward four-times-three
wise men with snowy alpine-peaking cowls.

Morning after morning all the way
        to Christmas we arrive to laugh and wince at these,
                the jolliest
bigot bedecked in sugar-candy Santa beard,

children in his lap, his kind face beaming behind us and before us
        everywhere in our mirrors—
                I'm ahead of myself—
off his lap go the innocents and one frame later

these girls and boys are dangling Christmas-present apes by nooses
        tied to Huck Finn bamboo
                fishing poles.
Our assembled jury is all leers, jeering

or are those cheers—I have the sound turned off—
        whose mouth
                is opening
to say this—just to look is abomination—

4

Outside is all look-see, so here again is the parking lot
      and its patron sparrow
            picking at a sodden
bread heel—

because it knows it can't carry the whole thing home
      it cocks its head at me and
            one eye staring at me
like a lapidary through a paste diamond,

it seems to see through all our jail-cell visions.
      I'm back, I never left—
            human snow outside,
human streets, I drive home past

skaters infesting frozen lakes, woolen ticks gliding
      on human ice, human gravitas
            scritching human circles.
I'm back on the treadmill,

someone I should know is behind and ahead of me running—

5

Here is the story of a queen- and king-size bed.
      The unknowable source is lonely for
            paradise,
car lights blow through God's voyeuristic head.

My guess is that anybody's eyes, when things get too hot,
      look away from the subject.
            Discursive
denies the erotic, narrative always ends up in the realm—

take a look—
of the postcoital—
but when she
touches me I'm home and so is she

and if the body's a prison cell,
we're clanking gold cups—
toasting our teeth to glass and ready for this good book
to open,

the silent nights after—
so so many.
God—look down on us—I don't have to tell you—
you are just as starved for us

as we are for ourselves.
A little warmth, a fire to read by, children, or not.
It is never death or the body
that degrades us,

it is that there have to be so many of us.

6

I leave when my thirty minutes of treadmill are up,
sparrow is there to see me
hauling towards its secret ends
my poor mortal god,

my body—
"young fellow" the old guy at the desk likes to call me.
There is so little to see
that will not be

looked upon and looked upon and looked upon—
      the old men from the pool who shamble their nakedness
         so carefully across
the cracked yellow tiles and past the scattered, almost

disintegrated bars of soap—past use.
      Their bodies steam like the street grates do.
        It is worth looking—
ice-coated windshields,

trees all snowy—clouds of unknowing—
      some berserk luminescence
        that persists
up and down so many lightsome streets.

And back inside, us, endless, speechless, running,
      dressing, undressing:
        us, steam,
the mirrors even, the potbellied mirrors—

it is worth looking—the sights outlive the sorrows.

Avenue of Vanishing

(1992–1995)

1

When the motors we've heard turn over for as long as childhood
hang clouds of exhaust dead or alive on driveways,
and the lawyer neighbor steps inside his car, quiet as a funeral,

and his wife walks to her private college library job,
a Walkman balanced in one palm like Augustine's *City of God*,
a cathedral buttressed by lasers so the songs and talk shows

can cross the glib green daybreak: dawn of spittle,
this surface health is mostly surface wealth.
Our neighborly squares of ChemLawn grass

are cobwebbed with these forms that first shoot through
a few square millimeters of arachnid neural cord
from some first distant reach success perfected,

all the way from the dawn of connection.
Trapdoor spiders leave to us their successful vortices.
Success has no head or time for sullenness or anger—

from the very dawn of want it spools our walks
between the house and the little liquor store.
Its late-Rothko window—neon's success at a signature.

And sometimes, often, no one in the aisles,
except for the clerk who may also have his habits—
see him, holding my twenty to the light

now, here, bountifully, exactly the way
people live on the strength of what they take from each other.

O

But it's dawn and the doors push back the light
before the light successfully comes in—.
Then the light was never there, shame on it.

The night comes in and walks right through our rec rooms.
In fog our house lights seem as jacklit fauna.
Houses brighten or darken, as faces darken

or brighten, one at a time, one at a time—
the way people die, or look up at the sky.
Success is like that and it is not like that:

that which happened in the sequel, termination of all affairs,
first wing brush and the subsequent spasms,
success without pause spooling out our days

past skateboards lying on their aching backs—

O

What is fortune but outward accident
for a few years sixty at most then gone,
said Blake, obliged to illustrate egg cups, tureens, crockeries, calling cards—

Fame if you win it lasts just a minute croons
Tony Bennett in "Make Someone Happy"—
and sometimes I do, you do, we smile past knowledge—

the neighbor's dog stops squealing like a saxophone
and I can stop trying not to pray for its death. *Mercy
to praise—to be forgiven for fame alone*—said Coleridge.

Mercy Mercy Me (Marvin Gaye) to understand whether it was fame
or something less addressable, some life buried out loud,
while it was breathing, Coleridge asked forgiveness for.

They say he learned how to talk even when he was asleep.
I've paged through lifetimes, through necrologies
with no words coming out of them that do not talk

of even better words: the words that got us here
may get us out of here but not our poorest failures—
long after success is finished looking out of us

success may have walked through the fire of success
and somehow not have been consumed
so that what is formed of the ashes can rise up to slay us.

O

Our neighbors and us, we're forced to talk sometimes
if it snows too hard, we're happy to, we unbury our cars
and even if the rest of the year we look away

it's partly in dejection we look away.
And "the purely reflective merely partakes of death. . . ."
The nearly undetectable derision of good friends,

rubbing each other the wrong way, disingenuous praise—
I feel more gone from the close friends than the far ones—
each trying to finish a book, a life, a family,

each success muttering clothe me, feed and fuck me,
each having to be pulled back from any boat
he made, if only to be made to enter that boat.

2

in the name of this organic and original naturalness
of the body we declare and wage war on drugs
—DERRIDA

What a life is the eye, Coleridge said.
It's good to romance the Romantics, a well-meaning
mistaken friend said (may she find true romance,

each instant boundless with necrologies . . .).
Or another friend who stole a numbered gravestone
and cleaned its beveled integers with a toothbrush—

her shrink said she was *taking care of herself.*
As for the widest friendship, it is a tiny town.
As for the world of *resist,* as for where we live now,

as for all these friends, only some of them forgot
us first, only some were put down in the books
in black-and-white, as we say when we want it in writing

because *God's rainbow will* is nothing I can read.
Because nature is another dawn unworldly and orange.
Because we hand ourselves perpetually

over to a night to which we are party—
Wasn't he a drug addict? Another friend.
He was I hear myself say. . . .

Cigarette smoke it'd take an axe to cut,
speaking animals tipping beers—
the Green Top Lounge, where we shall drink to our friends . . .

to be taken care of by nothing we can betray—
to friendship *addicted*—which once meant "devoted, bound, delivered
    over to"—
harsh success looks out at harsh success.

Across the street some kids pile out of a bus
to play rock'n'roll at a failed movie theatre.
These human amps for darkness dressed in black,

turn on the lights, faces of girls and boys say,
turn on the town, eyes open to bright night
and aren't the streetlights just as addicted,

glacial-slow police cars looking for easy fish,
the sulfur flaring in puddles we walk across
to the open coffin of our car—

○

*Crack Wars. In an altogether uncanny manner, the polemics surrounding drugs
historically become a War only when crack emerged. Crack lost its specificity as merely
one drug among others. As synecdoche of all drugs, crack illuminates an internal
dimension of polemos—opening the apocalyptic horizon of the politics of drugs.*
                                              —AVITAL RONNELL

Whatever we most fear, we mostly are.
Success this, success that. Coleridge took his life
for all that life was worth and still it was

a life like a zero of breath on a window.
It was like this small town's crack-infested life—
a prostitute talking a mile a minute,

pulling out a pliers-bent TV antenna for a pipe.
O but the single instance scarcely existed—
too poor, this one, for a glass pipe, her eyewhites crazed with capillaries,

branching out like the shaken oaks, and pipeheads
walking as the memory of elms
past the cinder block Powerhouse Church of God,

the Polar Bear Liquors with its neon polar bear,
the Beehive Foods, the Company Store—
just one hit—outside already inside—

occupied, everybody on the dotted line—
nullified to synecdoche, for now
the bar lights had spread filaments everywhere

and the night swung its censer of car exhaust,
streetlights stretching out an ellipsis. . . .
Crack, sheer success, the fast-food drug without

a speaker shaped like a clown to shout your order in,
cheese crumb for a mousetrap, the size of the "tiny"
you find in "infinity,"

a little revelation, something to put in the pipe.
Sometimes someone gets in and you go for a ride somewhere.
She took a hit, I breathed her spirit in me—

inhaled, and my life held her breath as I breathed in,
as the lights of night sparkling with lives inside
are all the dots there are for such as us to connect—

And it all comes back now: war zone: hapless success:
groups of dealers still and rustling as trees.
Once around the Northside to check for dragnets,

up Church, left on Patterson,
right on Cobb to North, right on North
to a left on to Park—nautilus-like involvulus

and orthogonal spiral—
to Westnedge, street named after a slaughtered colonel.
I'm driving down the avenue of vanishing—

that any pitiable individual instance
can scarcely exist at all,
an almost nonexistent fingernail-

dip into the tiny bag—what kind of shit am I—white shit—
immediately abstracted—peasanted—
occupied, every body on the dotted line—

no voice but this could come so close
to life without living into another—
everyone pulled their own face off—

the Pizza Hut neon was still on from the night before,
snowmelt shining on wet asphalt, more
falling from nowhere we can see, therefore

like some dedication utterly without beginning.
Pigeons eyelashing the Burger King sign.
Pigeons, unlike humankind, bear everything.

There I am, just like a human being:
humankind is not a very outgoing thought.
There, my profile—is it a signed confession?

She ripped me off, isn't that the American
way?—she broke off a piece from my chip
(me, what serious druggies call merely a chipper)

and set it next to her brother watching television.
It was a quiet offering, a charity,
it was as unsolicited as love,

it was my chip and it was smaller now.
Can we do better with our compassions or our prisons?
Drug dough cooked up in cookie pans,

it's a sad thing when you look at it
but whoever did, and now the law's involved,
now I can be arrested like an image,

immediately abstracted by pure need,
and suddenly feel a coroner's skin
draw tight upon my own,

—inside that place where no light shines
what thou hast entered here is thine
own now, no one else can get inside here. . . .

4

New stupefactions reel out of the dawn,
something in me looks up when the cat looks up and I still don't hear—
mostly survival is just not properly wired to hear.

That's success breathing life into all the passing faces,
success forgets the best idea of survival toward care it sometimes is,
new dawns eat away all other dawns,

and though each dawn is such good sight of our neighbors,
what we see is both there and not there,
just as our most substantial honesties are shadows,

are human and the cars don't sound like the ocean,
they don't unroll their sounds like Grecian scrolls,
they sound like tired voices stepped back off the docks again—

○

The spiders wait out flies in their guy-wired clouds of spit,
brocading the trapdoor webs also with moths
like dusty rooftops, and breakable deep grubs.

With day my neighbor drives off, his wife walks all the way
to her job of filing the good blindnesses of books,
their children drive to college and come back

like human boomerangs and are looking successful—
success is habit, and habit a policeable thoroughfare,
cop cars knifing each noon down our street.

For days and days I felt a coroner's skin
drawn tight upon my own. Now I shall be a lamb.
But not John Lamb, murdered murderer, Tex #587,

dead by the hand of the scabrous body politic—Nov. 10, 1999,
"It was almost as if I was shooting my bad luck or something."

○

I want a lullaby like a little bag.
I want a success I can breathe.
I want to star in a silent movie about a silence

that like all silence has no vocabulary to speak of.
I want to put down all my murdering wants
and feed them dog food for the rest of their hell.

The webs and the chain-link fences are where the daylight
is shining in dewdrop-bedecked barbed accordion wire
around the Mercedes dealership and the fast-talk salesmen,

hood ornaments, beautiful, untouchable, beyond my want,
light fortunate beyond all lullaby,
awake forever after in this past

which sometimes prays, but it's only blood that kneels,
every drop we've shed, or better, haven't, not
this time, this time, my little lies like lambs—

dawn again is the bread that crumbles softly
till another night shall reveal its handful of cares,
the spiders sleep, the stars sink to the human.

'TIS OF THEE

1

Play, we soldiered. Two Cub Scouts. Watched the stars
　　　and stripes fold in our hands,
　　　　　　triangle after triangle, every American
childhood afternoon,

two bearers brought
　　　nose to nose—
　　　　　　Jew. Protestant: me. . . . And Bob Salinger,
his every nasal word drew classmate smirks—

two bookish bookends apart from the fray
　　　above the "ditch," a runoff
　　　　　　where Yankee slaughtered
Rebel,

and that was only Recess—
　　　regimented stars,
　　　　　　wolfish wind flapped that fabricated firmament
to rags.

Above the White House One Whole Week
　　　it was said to have rippled,
　　　　　　a wing without another wing—
above the ersatz dead both blue and gray,

their hands waving
       in that gouge,
           —don't
drop it or let it touch the earth

or they'll never again let us near it—.

2

He couldn't even hit a tee-ball.
       The Cub Scout follows goodwill. Our school's tattered flag
           flew above his father's funeral service—
first neighbor

who made it to print, *Chicago Tribune*, first page,
       first death,
           suicide—don't—wingless from a high-rise
window on the Loop.

And there his family was—*flew nowhere*—a rabbi, Mrs. Bell
       the principal.
           The folding chairs on the school yard
older than most of us were.

Dung-colored metal chairs. One mourner moaned,
       her son whimpered—
           half-lives
I listened to and carried home.

○

Through two undeclared wars the boyish waged,
       through Bill after Bill of Wrongs,
           broken spirits, broken mothers, fathers, that flag
flew,

all my family flag's hangings
　　　　　hauled down and scissored into strips for the trash
　　　　　　　by my mother—
1970—

that here on memory's buffeted
　　　　　school yard of little wingless stars and a snotty-
　　　　　　　faced fatherless
child crying in assent to thee,

I can love her if only for tearing up
　　　　　our galaxy. Another Mother for Peace.
　　　　　　　Not her sons, they weren't
going to be killed

by time, or dope, or if the lottery
　　　　　didn't go your way,
　　　　　　　an inalienable
shell.

And there behind her on the idiot box
　　　　　was Abbie Hoffman on trial,
　　　　　　　in contempt for being the first to make our flag
a fashion statement.

His smirk broke into a smile.

○

Steal This Book. I took it out. Reading was theft enough.
　　　　　We read that back then as
　　　　　　　we read Thoreau, *Catch-*
22, Travels with Charlie, Look Homeward Angel,

the *Harvard Lampoon*—bedazzlement before
the public, published
word.
Our authors, our authorities

who delivered us from worse authorities
have flown now.
Our country has not died but certainly
has changed,

our parents
scarcely the mention of their own
existence,
our little mousy friends, our little mousy

posterities,
our sky of stars and stripes the eyes pry through, our wide,
blue-gray-welkin flag,
our in-every-way

literary,
moral, personal, historical,
cosmic,
quavering father-flag and mother- and sons- and daughters-flag

a brilliant presence hanging in the air,
tethered to mortal hands and eyes
our nothing-holds-long
flag,

our prêt-à-porter fashion flag, our what-is-the-sound-
of-one-death-of-a-businessman-dropping
flag,
our take-me-down-before-the-night-falls flag.

The Book of Love

In Hyde Park, on the gentle Rotten Row,
two lovers far from public in a public park
stroll so many years and streetlights ago.
She smiles at him, anew, ajar, a bit stark.

He thinks, do smiles come from very far.
They see the newspaper of some faceless
person open to its own obliviousness.
The Book of Generations never closes,

the Book of Lamentations never closes,
but open the Book of Love and all our cares
become a Song of Songs or an epic war
in a Book of Disappearances near and far

or else the Book of Memory won't open,
or else the Book of Love that no one knows
the end of won't open when arms open,
or else the book won't open, and it opens.

Frost's Last Lecture: A Tape: His Audience

(1963)

They are listening to what he hears. They are long ago.
They step into the lecture, it's never the same twice.

The cough, the rustle of a chair, the common laughter
breaking up, intake, labored pause, the obstinate sigh . . .

they are listening to what they heard and what he heard.
He seems too lost in his notes to go the rest of the way.

Let them go to the wolves, he said of those who can't keep up.
You could almost hear those wolves, their shatter-breath.

The gist seems always so, clear, if anything is clear.
One sentence at a time, he keeps saying goodbye. . . .

Don't sympathize with it too much an old voice said.
Extravagance is meager acts and subtler inactions,

pursuit or escape, of the broken world, broken love.
Ordained or not, they've failed, it must be made better.

But first they must freely submit to their essence and
all over again ENDURE their freedom: extravagance:

sometimes it's remorse, sometimes it's nearly hope,
sometimes it's something they couldn't bear to hope.

PART

FOUR

○

Rag for the Prayer-Rag Tree

(Madron)

The rags of missing peoples mock us in a little wind:
rags, and shoes, and potpourri have inherited the tree,
this blue mitten, that stained green lace strip, this yellow curtain strip of
    crescent moons
and other curtain strips hanging practically on air,
blue shoe string, red-black threaded boot string, two baby shoes turning just
    like rowboats.
This tree of perpetual arrival, a shoe tree, is one more life to pray for.
On this tree of Things That No One Wants, on this pompon of prayers
some rags flutter in the gray sea wind and blow sometimes all the way to the
    Irish Sea,
other rags hang on and can't fall, and these make us the sorriest.
Here's one finger of a wedding glove . . . what love will do to leave even
    a trace.
This tree bandaged by moss, onto which prayers are lashed, has rags for
    winter leaves.
Its winter shade a trash-shade cast by trash,
this tree going nowhere has a luggage tag with no return address for no
    luggage
and a Magic Tree Deodorizer and a thumbnail-sized Buddha at the bottom of
a dope baggie
filled with water, eyes wide obeying its nature like a child,
gulls blowing around like the litter they eat as to never entirely blow
    away.
These things no one particularly loves, things once we had, and held,

hang on the drab wish of all prayer, for prayer to cease to be—
rags tied tight on this tree for pagans and Christians and Wiccans,
this multitudinous tree where we rid ourselves of our shoestring
    prayers.
Here's the lowliest, a raindrop-scourged violet thread, ghost of a string,
a shoestring wraith tied to the lowest twig to trouble the holy waters—
how does sunlight, how do our shadows not get blown away when it's this
    windy?
What is the prayer for such a tree, what new trash can we tie to this tree of
    trash?
It can't require much strength for me to rent this rag and tie it tight and leave
    with one less prayer.

BEDSIDE

Because it turns out the world really is a hospital,
Because we had to have had before us a giant pair of scissors
Before four bold wings can have newly ascended,
Before new doors can revolve, before new elevators
Rise and fall empty and full, new numbers light,
New floors with new doors both open and closed
Because there are nurses to sail in and out of need,
Because need walks the doctors somewhere or another,
Because of elaborately adaptable need the bed . . .
The bed could be wheeled right into traffic and snow
Because so far there is only inside and outside
And more of both than even creation could have concocted,
Because the bed that bore us all and our desires
And our exhaustions has become a contraption,
Because the bed that keeps us coming back to it,
The bed that once sailed to the ends of the earth—
Now tied to trees dripping blood and sugar and sleep,
Anchored where overhead a TV persists, such news
As snows poor reception—because the reliable bed
Is something even a family understands, the family
Is how the world goes—a fool's dream of awareness—
Grouped around this steel altar at its least and lowered
Because the bed is a helpless, blameless invention,
All the same to it if it is made or not, empty or not,
Same fatiguing last probabilities, because there are
As many ways to die as people to find these ways
Because there surely are, because the tried is ever new,

Who can't lose their way anew among so many alive?
Because who hasn't made their own bed, because
Who hasn't slept who hasn't been led by night there,
My mother's hands playing the fabric of the spread
As if it were a piano, tongue-tied, isolate fingers,
She's ghost-smoking, working on an invisible crochet
"Hate Hate Hate Hate Hate . . . I want to die"—
"Wake up!" Machado said the Gospels reduced to
But not now, not until you have what you want—
Any belief in love itself is what I'd have you want—
Look me in the eye with that sort of love that looks
Through me as if grief were so much tissue paper,
With a love that doesn't stop with me or you, that
Doesn't stop when there's no more world to fear
Because there is no need to wheel the bed outside,
Because a hospital melts like a snowflake, because
The walls and windows and even the bed liquify,
Even the things she's seen that aren't there vanish
Because how much energy there is in emptiness,
Take everything away, there's still something there.

Universe of Fear

. . . to replace the world with a universe of fear
—E. M. CIORAN

You can't push back the darkness with a gun.

O

You can't bomb the darkness or the darkness has won.

O

But you can have your deathday in the open.

O

You can die back into singular men and women.

O

Beware of those who worship sacrifice.

O

They'll grind you *into dust.* Their love is ice.

O

Banish the "I" and what do the ayes have?

O

Nothing they or we or you can starve or save.

O

Let THEIR dead *just try* to bury OUR dead:

O

Choice is NEVER ours: it's in our head:

O

May the weak FEED on public imperative.

O

Die for freedom. Freedom lives to grieve.

O

Grieve for the living. Pray even for the leaf.

O

Theorize CHAOS. Grieve. Justice is strife.

O

Make a house of cardboard. It is life.

O

Life is everyone's. TAKE no purity.

○

Escape from escape. There is no security.

○

There's no inside until you step outside:

○

Where not a hair lives that you can hide,

○

Not a wish that isn't crushed out loud

○

Or a twig that isn't firewood for need.

○

Burn out loud now everything once safe

○

Is trembling, ashen, and beyond belief.

False Rue

(April)

Out of everything, we most dread the causes,
and the green creaks again and we are here,
about to embark on the lifeboat of an ear,
about to descend by the lifeline of a fear
to study disenfranchised spring beauties,
meadow of trillium with spring at the tip of their hesitant lips,
language among the first to become visible.
Winter slammed and slammed and . . . *couldn't,*
geese honking—like an ample barn door opening.
The unlikelihood of the actual shames us silent.
And silence has no vocabulary to speak of
this April in us, this change come over us,
nature avenging us for thinking it cruel by going
under, and then it had never been there, shame on it,
shame on a hat of snow on the wasp's nest,
shame on us, our craven praise and odal joy,
shame on exquisite metaphors that made us hurt both more and less.
So on we go back to slaughter the weaker words,
the way we slaughtered the wasps, little spacemen,
larval, unincubated, squirming out of their lives
of which there were so many we shall have to poison.
Even in a language of utmost care the world
disappears and yet so guilelessly the words
we haven't killed yet lie down and weep for us,
marigolds dash themselves against the stones,

no matter this brainless filth and murk and dirt,
the names themselves come up, list south, slope to false rue,
by the waters of Babylon the words lie down—
by the tracks of a train for warehouses of coal—
weeping for us whose voices leave the world,
we the worriers of our world, its venting selves
required to leave the world because the world says
we know we can't take care of everything, but
it gets harder and harder to feel okay about the mess
we're leaving the world to our edible children,
and somehow this anxiety isn't perfectly ennobling,
we don't have a name for every thought we think
to fight off the last thought, we walk along water,
seeking a near transparency in the selvage.
And in the newts first evasions become apparent,
and the first to come the hepatica the first to go,
these augurs, fixed limitations without which
there would be no room for more of these perishables,
these hardihoods pushing up through loam,
up through the stale grandeur of annihilation—
spring must be trying to get over its addiction
to everything. Spring is all about our famed
futures that feed like Ugolino on his children.
We don't feel properly introduced to our loved ones
till we have lost them, till we believe we have.
We wrote down spring in journals all ice that melted,
while spring rubbed its face blue with the understanding
that spring is the undertaking of the overtaken,
spring is that no one can survive this world,
spring is that this foison bears helplessness,
spring is waking from a coma to gnats without number,
no one can survive this world in common.
Spring is our own excellent luck larger than our eyes,
our eyes that do not on their own tyrannize,
listing flowers for a prayer trance preying on lists,

up from some kind of halfway house all shameless,
misidentifications and misbegotten identifications,
one person's trout lily another person's adder's-tongue,
the bloodroot blossom's infantile pinwheel petals
and moose-antler jigsaw leaves a child must have drawn,
yellow squirrel corn, wanton Dutchman's-breeches,
early splurge, wild tease so sight can see such shove,
trillium white as the inside of a halved potato,
white of the human skull that houses all reverence,
sub-rosa white of the mayapples' chthonic knobs
shoving their light into light and the famishing rain,
white-faced as a god who suddenly recalls mortality.
These flowers have had to go to Antarctica and back.
We may not feel the seasons at all the same as they
though the same turbulence lives us to mutual ends,
last leaves on beech saplings—flocks stalled
metallic yellow—long over their revulsion to gravity,
two mallards circling a pond ten times or more
to drop with our very eyesight out of eyesight
below the stand of beech still bare and articulate,
below sucking muskegs the honesties live through,
below our pity on others that divides the soul,
below trampled muckland that is a filthy grace,
skunk cabbages unscrolling their stink for early bees,
the shepherd's purse, the bouncing bet drawn up from
where there is no ample excruciating punishment,
where winter was only a gate that slammed and slammed
and still couldn't close on mud and murk and dirt,
where the way back up is neither simply night nor day,
where we were made of substance, it is not secret,
where, just when disbelief craves the very last word,
gone is anything greater than this outrageous green.

CREATION ASSUMES THE FORM OF WASHED-UP KELP

What it must have taken
to be let loose
along the cataloguing shore,
floating congregations

throwing nowhere ropes
to nobody and no one
and beaching entwined,
this being intimacy,

this being entanglement,
umbilical from head to toe—
everything connects—
beyond our embrace,

calypso mop-tops,
freaked dumpsites
fretted and dinged,
vast chain gangs

of common criminals,
each sentence ending
in a dim-bulb brain
while perdurable pebbles

create little scratchy
radio transmitter sounds,
the sea's Shiva-arms
reaching out even when

there's no hand to hold.
Only a stink unfolds
from the sand-beaded holdfasts
that invite all likeness

and defy all likeness
and sleep in themselves
and string us along.
And drool over all

human comparison—
stipes flute-stopped with dints,
the blubbery wings,
water if you look long,

seersucker seamstered,
bunched at the verges,
a dirty laundry pile
of worldly citizens

we test with the tips
of our steel toes,
burst the bloated blobbers,
heel the languished

with our furious intentions
to walk across water,
leave the world behind
and beneath the gnat,

see one sight so right
it annihilates all subsequence,
till nothing is there
but one brainlessly

cranial, mental jellyfish,
and nothing is lost
except such as these
as cannot move us

unless they hold us
by having let us go
and having themselves
made landfall here

and there where the sea
groans beneath them,
beneath and beyond
each and every elsewhere—

—where else on earth
would we place these,
past our grasp,
all this catastrophe?

A Fallen Bat

Little fanfare, mute echo with a shrunken head,
Shrewlike glider Linnaeus lumped with the humans,

I do not for our big world know where life ends
But you should be up there swarming the stars.

Leaf-nosed hand wing, unheard-music screamer,
Flexogram, wall-sticker, scooper of linear bees,

Black bud not even the noon light can blow out,
Wherever life ends it doesn't have to end tonight.

It only gets worse, cave dweller, pollen carrier.
It simply will not do to play dead forever after.

Madame Midnight, St. Nick, Nostradamus, Nosferatu,
Death and Hell would be hard put to swallow you.

Little wet pill, please rise to wherever it is you rise.
Scream back at your own ears if you have a choice.

It's now or never, moreover, and just as well,
Life or death, mercy or murder, care or fear.

Stunned umbrella, unfold the night, make it keen.
Before I die I want to be a ledge you can hang

For all your life to, long before I die I want to say
Not yet. Even if nobody asks, fanged voice.

Torment, blind necessity, break my eardrums,
Dearest ash, but not before the time has come.

Phone Book

It is all reasonable
and unreasonable
inside this book I understand
just about as well

as I do my body—
it's not dust yet.
I look both ways
crossing its streets,

its stricken pages,
almost by heart.
Its nighthawks—
that's how edgy

the body sounds
when it flies
between buildings.
If only for night

yellow streetlights
come on, stay lit
like need on a face,
lamp on this book.

Across the street
foglight rolls
looking both ways
like I do when

I turn the pages,
lifetimes roll,
everyone is here,
anyone can see

the barbershops
are closed for the day—
honest mirrors,
faceless as fears,

staring as if alive—
the rotating thrones,
resolute steel,
look royally lost.

More pages turn,
on every last one
are addresses
to tell me where

all the others are—
alphabetized names—
families rhyme
yet perhaps not

one knows another.
There turn the motels,
there the car lots,
clean restaurants

on yellow pages,
lamplight on faces,
leaves on the night,
wind in the leaves.

In the fearless book
of fears what rolls
over rolls over by heart,
the unstaunched

stoplight turns
emerald by heart,
everyone is on
their way home

or away from home,
everyone knows
just how far from
the beginning we are,

streets of emptiness,
streets of business,
our little universe.
This book can't take us

anywhere but here,
this scrawny sky
nighthawks scrawl—
not one cry has to

be reminded to carry.
Every street's here.
Thunderous trucks.
Our and every face

or name or number,
every call or voice,
every untold house,
every phantom grace.

Notes

"Sotto Voce"
The phrase quoted in line 58 is from W. S. Merwin's "Some Last Questions."

"Avenue of Vanishing"
Line 30 in section 4 adapts a phrase from a letter by W. S. Graham. The phrase
is reprised in "False Rue."

"Bedside"
The last line of the poem derives from a statement the physicist Lawrence
Krauss made about empty space.

About the Author

William Olsen is a professor at Western Michigan University and Vermont College. He has received fellowships from the Guggenheim Foundation, the National Endowment for the Arts, and Breadloaf. His three previous collections of poetry are *The Hand of God and a Few Bright Flowers*, *Vision of a Storm Cloud*, and *Trouble Lights*. He lives in Kalamazoo.